# OLYMPIC
## National Park

**by Ruth Radlauer**

**Design and photographs
by Rolf Zillmer**

AN ELK GROVE BOOK

 CHILDRENS PRESS, CHICAGO

The author thanks the personnel
of Olympic National Park
for assistance with photography
and authentication of the manuscript.

**Cover Photo: Hall Of Mosses—Hoh Rain Forest**

Library of Congress Cataloging in Publication Data
Radlauer, Ruth Shaw.
  Olympic National Park.
  (Parks for people)
  "An Elk Grove book."
  SUMMARY: Describes the physical features, plant and
animal life, and camping accommodations in this
Washington State park of high mountains, rain forests,
and seacoast.
  1. Olympic National Park—Juvenile literature.
[1. Olympic National Park. 2. National parks and
reserves] I. Zillmer, Rolf. II. Title.
F897.05R32      917.97'94      77-5836
ISBN 0-516-07494-6

# Contents

# What is Olympic National Park?

Olympic National Park is three parks in one: high mountains, rain forests, and a seacoast.

At the seacoast, this park is the rushing of ocean waves on the sand. It's the lonely call of gulls looking for food in the water. Mysterious rocks, the sea stacks, stand among driftwood thrown on the beach by the waves. Here you can see starfish on the rocks of a tide pool.

A cool, green rain forest grows thick in the valleys. You can walk through this forest and gaze at huge trees and tiny mosses. You'll see small trees growing on a nurselog, the old trunk of a fallen tree. Many ferns, mosses, and lichens grow in this wet, green world.

Your family can drive to the high mountains on Hurricane Ridge Road. At the end of the road, an easy trail takes you up Hurricane Hill. As you get above the tree line, mountain meadows may be white with avalanche lilies, or blue with lupine. Watch for a furry ball of life the size of a small dog. When you hear the Olympic marmot's whistle, you'll know you've arrived at Olympic National Park.

Sea Stacks At Ruby Beach

Sea Star (Starfish)

Maidenhair Fern

Mt. Carrie From Hurricane Ridge

Olympic Marmots

# Where is Olympic National Park?

Olympic National Park is in the northwest corner of Washington State. You can get there on a ferryboat from Victoria, B. C., Canada, to Port Angeles, Washington. Some people fly to Seattle and take a smaller plane or a bus to Port Angeles.

By car, visitors drive to Seattle and take a ferryboat to Highway 101 which loops around the park.

This park has 16 campgrounds with 934 campsites. Most of them have tables, cooking fireplaces, and restrooms.

For information about campgrounds, cabins, and trailer parks, write to the Superintendent, 600 East Park Avenue, Port Angeles, Washington 98362, and Olympic Resort and Hotel Association, Seattle Ferry Terminal, Seattle, Washington, 98104.

If you plan to camp overnight along the park's trail system, you need a backcountry use permit. You'll also want a backpack, a small camp stove, a tent, and a sleeping bag.

Whatever you plan to do in the park, your visit will be more fun if you take a raincoat or waterproof poncho, rubber boots, and maybe even an umbrella.

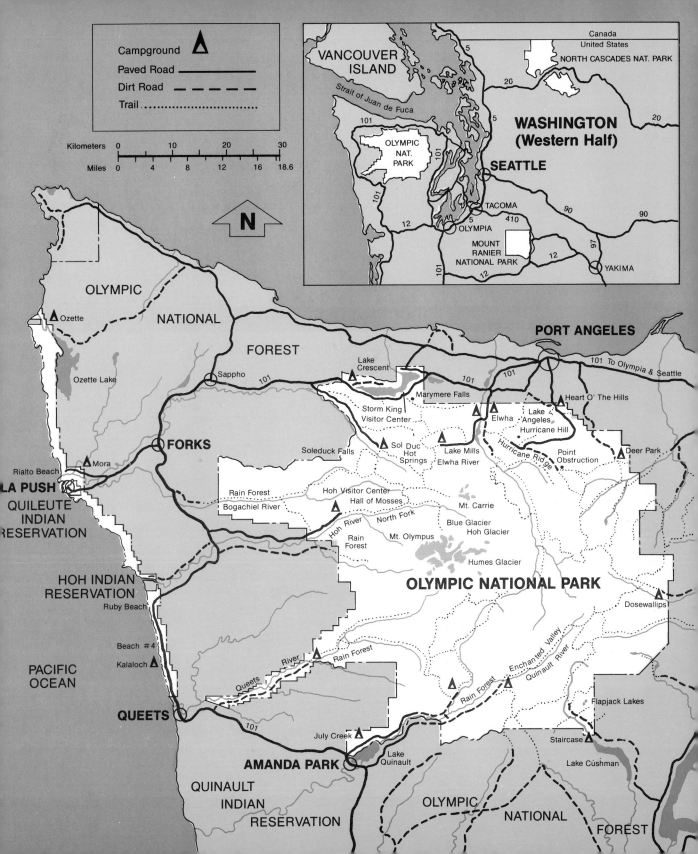

Campground ▲
Paved Road ——————
Dirt Road – – – – –
Trail ............................

Kilometers  0    10    20    30
Miles  0   4   8   12   16   18.6

N

**WASHINGTON**
(Western Half)

Canada
United States

VANCOUVER
ISLAND

NORTH CASCADES NAT. PARK

Strait of Juan de Fuca

5

20

20

5

101

101

OLYMPIC
NAT.
PARK

101

**SEATTLE**

TACOMA

90

90

12

5

410

OLYMPIA

MOUNT
RANIER
NATIONAL
PARK

97

YAKIMA

12

101

12

OLYMPIC

NATIONAL

FOREST

▲ Ozette

Ozette Lake

Sappho

101

Lake
Crescent

Marymere Falls

**PORT ANGELES**

101

101    To Olympia & Seattle

Heart O' The Hills ▲

Storm King
Visitor Center

Soleduck Falls

Sol Duc ▲
Hot
Springs

▲ ▲ Elwha
Lake
Angeles
Hurricane Hill

Lake Mills ▲
Elwha River

Hurricane Ridge

Point
Obstruction

Deer Park ▲

**FORKS**

Rialto Beach

▲ Mora

**LA PUSH**

QUILEUTE
INDIAN
RESERVATION

Rain Forest
Bogachiel River

Hoh Visitor Center
Hall of Mosses ▲

Hoh River    North Fork

Rain
Forest

Mt. Carrie

Blue Glacier
Hoh Glacier

Mt. Olympus

Humes Glacier

**OLYMPIC NATIONAL PARK**

Dosewallips ▲

HOH INDIAN
RESERVATION

Ruby Beach

Beach #4

Kalaloch ▲

PACIFIC
OCEAN

Queets    River

Rain Forest ▲

Enchanted Valley
Quinault River

Rain Forest ▲    ▲

Flapjack Lakes

Staircase ▲

**QUEETS**

101

July Creek ▲

**AMANDA PARK**

Lake
Quinault

Lake Cushman

QUINAULT

INDIAN

RESERVATION

OLYMPIC    NATIONAL    FOREST

# Water, Water, Everywhere

Olympic National Park is a gift of the water cycle. Ocean water on the surface of a warm sea evaporates and turns into a gas you can not see. The gas is called water vapor. Wind from the west carries the water vapor toward the mountains.

All air cools as it rises, but this air from the west is cooled even faster as it flows up over the cold Olympic Mountains. When water vapor cools, it turns into the mist of clouds, and finally into droplets that fall to earth as raindrops. Very cold droplets turn to ice and form snowflakes.

Rain and snow are called *precipitation*. About two meters of yearly precipitation make it possible for millions of trees to grow in the lowland forests near the ocean. Higher up, about four meters of precipitation fall on the wide valleys where rain forests grow. Way up on Mount Olympus, a year's precipitation is about five meters.

The high mountain rain and melting snow feed many streams. The streams rush over waterfalls and gather into wide rivers that find their way to the ocean.

This cycle has no real beginning or end, but goes on and on and on.

**Water Vapor Rises And Turns Into Clouds**

**Marymere Falls**

**Rivers Flow Out To Sea**

**Streams Of Rainfall And Melting Snow Flow Down The Mountain**

# Tide Pool Walk

When you visit Olympic National Park's beaches at Kalaloch or Mora, you can go on a Tide Pool Walk with a Ranger. Tide pools are pockets of water that stay among the rocks during low tide. These pools allow some animals to live closer to the shore where you can see them when the tide is low.

Animals in a tide pool cling to the rocks with strong "feet." Under the five arms of the common sea star, or starfish, are many tiny tube feet. The sea star breathes, feels things, and clings with its tube feet. During low tide you'll find sea stars among sea anemones.

When water covers the green or pink anemones, their tentacles flower out, waiting for food to come along. Out of water, this beautiful animal folds its tentacles into itself and looks like a dimpled blob of mud stuck to the rock.

Dungeness and other crabs live in eel-grass beds or in sand under deeper water. When a crab grows too big for its shell, it molts. It breaks out of its shell and forms a new one. As you walk along the beach, you may find an empty shell left after a crab molts.

**Tide Pool Walk With A Ranger**

**Sea Star Among Sea Anemones**

**Dungeness Crab**

# Beach Fun

Low tide comes at different times every day. If you read the free park newspaper, you'll know where and when to meet a Ranger for a Tide Pool Walk.

On your own you can have other beach fun as long as you keep an eye on the waves. Especially during storms, the waves throw big logs up on the beach, and one could surprise you at any time. Some of these logs are from barges carrying wood to lumber mills. Most of them are trees washed into the sea by rivers in the forests.

At the beach you can walk on the sand and play tag with the waves or watch bunches of sandpipers as they scurry along the water's edge.

Some people like to climb on the rocks during low tide or build castles with wet sand.

About the time the sun sets, you can go to the beach campfire below Kalaloch Campground. As you watch the flames reaching into the starry sky, the Ranger tells about life in the tide pool, or about the history of Olympic National Park.

**Climb On The Rocks**

**Build Sand Castles**

# Birds

Many kinds of birds visit or live in Olympic National Park. The easiest ones to see are those along the seashore.

The bald eagle lives on cliffs by beaches where few people go. Hikers may spot one soaring high above the water. If an eagle sees a fish, it drops to the water and grabs it with sharp talons. Then it flies away to a tree to eat. But sometimes an eagle never gets to eat its catch, because bunches of ravens gang up and rob the eagle in flight.

Cormorants are great fishers. These big black birds can swim under water. They often plunge through the tops of waves to feed on fish. Watch for these long-necked birds nesting on sea stacks at Ruby and Rialto Beaches. Their feathers are not waterproof, so you may see their wings spread out to dry.

Gulls soar over the water, swim, or walk on the beach. When many gulls gather and hover over the surf, people know the small fish called smelt are there. The smelt are coming to lay their eggs on a beach of coarse sand. So smelters get out their big nets and try their luck at smelting.

**Cormorants At Rialto Beach**

**Gulls**

**Smelting**

# Trees-
# Lowland
# Forest

At Kalaloch Beach Campground, you can meet with a Ranger for a walk through the lowland forest. On the walk you learn that forests usually have levels, or stories. Close to the ground is the first story where low plants and seedling shrubs grow. Higher off the ground, young trees and shrubs grow on the second level. The third story has bigger trees, and the biggest trees make the fourth story. This story forms a covering, or canopy, over the others.

In this wet lowland forest, the canopy lets very little sunlight reach the ground. Only shade-loving trees do well here. They are the western redcedar, western hemlock, and sitka spruce.

A busy animal kingdom works in the lowland forest. Insects like termites, wood beetles, and carpenter ants clean up the forest by eating dead leaves and wood.

If you see something that looks like a pile of sawdust, it's the chickaree's trash pile. The chickaree, or Douglas squirrel, cuts down sitka spruce cones and eats the seeds. It leaves the scales and cores of the cones in a pile under the tree.

**Western Hemlock Droops Beside A Douglas-Fir**

**Western Redcedar Leaves Are Scales Along The Twigs**

**Hemlock Needles Are Short, Flat, And Soft**

**Chickaree**

# The Lowest and Slowest

In forests below 500 meters elevation, you may come upon a very strange greenish yellow creature with spots. Bigger than most garden slugs, it's the banana slug.

You can pick up this animal carefully and take a good look. The slug has two pairs of antennae. The long upper antennae are used to sense light. The lower antennae, at each side of the mouth, sense smells. Can you think why such an animal needs to be able to smell?

On the slug's right side is a small hole. When the slug gets used to you, you may see the hole open and close as the animal breathes. Looking at the underside, you'll see a rippling muscle that makes the banana slug move along. When you put it down, the slug breaks no speed limits as it slowly oozes away, leaving a trail of thick slippery liquid, or mucus. (Try not to get the mucus on your fingers, unless you want to glue them together.)

Along with the black slug, this one eats decaying things like dead leaves and bark, or debris. As the debris passes through the slug's body, it turns into good soil. You see, even the lowest and slowest creature in the forest is important.

**Banana Slug — About 1½ Times Life Size** ▶

# Trees – Rain Forest

Up from the seacoast are the wide valleys carved by glaciers. Mountain snows melt into these valleys already drenched by more than three meters of yearly rainfall.

Giant trees stand tall in this rain forest. The soil is soggy with water, so roots spread out. No need to sink a taproot deep into the ground for water. But without a taproot to anchor them, these trees sometimes fall when a strong wind blows. A fallen tree becomes a nurselog as it dies and begins to decay.

Seeds that could never sprout in the thick mat of the lower story can sprout when they fall on a nurselog. Seedling trees sink their roots into the log and grow very slowly for about 20 or 30 years. At the same time, a few roots trail over the log seeking soil. When their roots finally reach the soil, the trees get more food, or nutrients, and begin to grow faster. Many years later, the nurselog is completely hidden under the huge roots of towering trees that grow in a row called a colonnade.

It can take as long as 700 years from the time a tree dies until a colonnade grows where its trunk fell to the ground.

**Seedlings Grow On A Nurselog**

**Colonnade—The Work Of Centuries**

# Ferns and Mosses

You can get to know the rain forest when you join a Guided Forest Walk at the Hoh Rain Forest Visitor Center. During this two-hour stroll, you get a chance to look closely at nurselogs, nurse stumps, ferns, mosses, and lichens.

You find out those little dark bits on the back of fern leaves, or fronds, are spore cases. When the spores are ripe, the cases open, and the spores fall to the ground. They grow into tiny plants that produce new ferns.

High in a spruce or bigleaf maple tree is a licorice fern. It's an epiphyte, a plant that hangs onto another plant. An epiphyte gets its nutrients from dust in the air or debris that falls on it.

There are 71 species, or kinds, of mosses growing in the rain forest. They grow on the ground, on nurselogs, or up high as epiphytes.

After your Guided Forest Walk, you'll enjoy a quiet walk through the Hall of Mosses. Here you'll find you can name many of the new plants you learned about from the Ranger.

The rain forest is a soft green place, a place to listen, a place to feel the wonder of how life goes on and on.

**Spores On A Sword Fern**

**Licorice Fern, An Epiphyte**

**Hall Of Mosses**

# Lichens

A lichen is a combination of two plants: a fungus and an alga. The fungus holds water and gives the plant its shape and hardness. The alga makes food for both of them. To make food, the alga uses water, sunlight and carbon dioxide, a gas in the air.

In many different shapes and colors, lichens grow on tree bark and branches, rocks, and nurselogs.

You'll see many kinds of lichens in the lowland forest and the rain forest. When they grow on the trunk of a red alder, the bark looks silver instead of red.

You must look closely to see the lacy lichen that grows on the branches of bigleaf maple trees.

Lichens and mosses are the first plants to grow on a nurselog. But a hemlock or spruce log may have been on the ground as long as 100 years before these "pioneer plants" begin to grow on it. And it takes a redcedar or Douglas-fir log as much as 500 years to decay and soften enough for new plants to take root on it. It's fun to imagine what was happening in the world when one of these giants fell.

**Lichen Turns Red Alder Bark Silver**

**Lichen On Bigleaf Maple**

# Gardeners with Antlers

Two members of the deer family live in Olympic National Park: the black-tailed deer and the Olympic elk.

A female elk is called a cow, and a female deer is a doe. Only males have antlers. Bull elk and buck deer shed their antlers every year after mating season. About two weeks after a male sheds its antlers, small furry bumps form on the stubs left by the old antlers. These soft, puffy balls are full of circulating blood. It circulates through the antlers as long as they grow. While they grow, antlers are covered with a furry skin, or velvet.

When antlers stop growing, the blood stops circulating through them. They harden and the velvet peels off.

Look for signs of elk and deer in the rain forest. They rub their antlers on trees to get the velvet off. You may see rubbed-off bark or furry bits of skin clinging to a tree.

You may also see signs of their "gardening." Sometimes called "the gardeners of the rain forest," their browsing on shrubs and young trees keeps the lower stories of the rain forest open to sunlight.

**Buck Deer In Velvet**

**Olympic Elk Female, Or Cow**

# How is a Mountain?

People who study the earth and what it's made of are geologists. Geologists believe the earth is covered with a crust about 65 kilometers thick. The crust is made up of huge irregular pieces called "plates."

The earth's plates float on very hot, melted rock called magma. Floating on the magma, the plates move very slowly. One plate may slip under another and cause it to rise. At the same time, top layers of the plates break and pile up between them.

Millions of years ago, this part of the North American plate was a flat area made up of many layers of rock laid down in an ancient sea. Here and there magma in the form of lava had oozed up through cracks into the water. The lava cooled quickly in the water and formed blobs of rock called pillow lava.

When a plate to the west of Washington pushed against the North American plate, these layered rocks tilted. For the last 70 million years the Olympic Mountains have risen very slowly until the highest peaks are over 2400 meters high.

As you travel around the park, you may see pillow lava and tilted layers of the earth's crust.

Olympic Mountains Reach Over 2400 Meters High

Tilted Layers At Beach Number Four

Pillow Lava

# Mountains Change

Mountains change. The rocks are worn, or eroded away by plants, rain, snow, and ice.

When snow piles up year after year without a chance to melt, the bottom of it packs into ice. During the Ice Age, snow and ice filled whole canyons in the mountains of North America. These huge hunks of ice called glaciers slid down the slopes and gouged out the wide valleys where rain forests now grow.

Sometimes glaciers carve dish-like areas where they melt and form lakes, or tarns, such as Lake Angeles and Flapjack Lakes.

About 60 small glaciers are still at work changing the shape of the Olympic Mountains. Behind the lodge at Hurricane Ridge, you can look through a telescope to see some of them. The closest is Carrie Glacier on Mt. Carrie. Beyond, on Mt. Olympus are Humes, Hoh, and Blue Glaciers.

Backcountry hikers get a good look at Blue Glacier from the High Divide Trail. They can get to Anderson Glacier on the Dosewallips River Trail. But it takes special skill to go on a glacier. Climbers need crampons to wear on their feet, ropes, and ice axes for this kind of hiking.

**Glacier On Mt. Carrie**

# -and
# More Trees

As the clouds move up the side of the Olympic Range, they drop most of their water on the west side of the mountains. Every year the peaks get as much as five meters of precipitation. But east and north of the peaks, the land is drier.

On a drive up Hurricane Ridge Road, you can see how different plants grow at different elevations. At lower elevations between 460 and 770 meters, smaller trees like western white pine and Pacific silver fir turn the hills a darker green.

Higher, mountain hemlock, alpine fir, and Alaska cedar struggle to live in the windy cold. The earth is frozen solid much of the time. A shallow top layer of sandy soil doesn't hold water, and most of the precipitation flows down to the rich valleys below.

A short warm season means trees can only grow about four months a year. Near the tree line, or timberline, alpine firs cluster together in families. In family groups they protect each other from the wind. Their dark needles absorb the sun's energy and give off warmth to each other. Watch for these alpine families at Hurricane Ridge.

**Alpine Firs Grow In Families At High Elevations** ▶

# Hurricane Ridge Wild Flowers

Wild flowers grow at all elevations. In sunny places, especially along the roads, the tall fireweed nods its purple blossoms as you drive by.

High in mountain meadows the cool clear air smells like sweet peas when the subalpine lupine blooms. In midsummer it mixes with paintbrush to make a blue meadow dotted with red.

Avalanche lilies make seas of white stars in the meadows of Hurricane Hill and along the road to Obstruction Point. The white sea ripples as a breeze passes by. When you look closely you see stamens, heavy with yellow pollen, drooping from the center of each starlike face. Late in July, as they near the end of blooming, avalanche lilies turn a pale lavender.

But flowers of these high meadows do more than paint the slopes and make the meadows smell sweet. The sitka valerian, avalanche lily, lupine, and spreading phlox are important parts of the food supply for the Olympic marmot. These furry rodents eat flowers, herbs, and grasslike plants called sedges. The marmot's body stores the energy of these plants in body fat.

**Lupine And Paintbrush**

**Avalanche Lily**

# Olympic Marmot

Summers are short and winters are long in Olympic National Park. In the short growing season from late spring through summer, the Olympic marmot must eat all the food it can find.

When plenty of precipitation makes plenty of plants for food, marmots can store enough energy to get through the long Olympic winter. They also get through the winter better when deep snow acts as a thick blanket over their burrows in the ground.

When there is no more food to eat, marmots go into their burrows to hibernate. During hibernation, an animal's breathing rate and heartbeat slow down. The body is in a very deep sleep and uses very little energy.

The Olympic marmot hibernates seven or eight months a year. Other marmots east of the Cascade Mountains hibernate between four and seven months a year.

If you think you hear the bark of a French poodle as you hike up Hurricane Hill, look across the meadow. It may be the Olympic marmot announcing the approach of some two-legged animals, such as you and your friends.

**Olympic Marmot**

**Olympic Marmot**

# Wilderness– Enjoy It

Roads take you all around Olympic National Park, but trails will take you into its wilderness. If you want to go camping in the backcountry or backpack on the beach, you need a wilderness permit. You can get a free permit at any Ranger Station or Visitor Center. The Ranger will help you plan your trip, talk about beach and mountain safety, and tell you what equipment you need.

A small, lightweight stove will cook your food much better than a wood fire. In many places, wood fires are not allowed, and sometimes you can't find dry wood.

You may see some wild animals when you visit their home in the backcountry. Some animals may look friendly, but remember, they're wild. Especially dangerous is a mother with young to protect.

It's also dangerous and against the law to feed wild animals, even squirrels. Your cooking smells may attract hungry bears. Rangers say to put all food in your pack at night and hang it very high on a rope between two trees. Try to tie the rope ends out of the bear's reach.

Write the Superintendent for information to help you plan to enjoy your wilderness. (Address on page 6.)

**Visitors See Rain Gear And Taste Freeze-Dried Food**

**Hang Food High In The Air**

# Rain-Enjoy It

"Rain, rain, go away." That's what some people say when they get to Olympic National Park. But think what this wonderland would be like without rain.

That important water cycle makes this national park what it is. So why not enjoy the rain? You can enjoy rain if you expect it and prepare for it.

Rain pants and jacket are good for short walks. But they don't let water in *or* out. This means, on a hard hike, you may get wet from the inside when you sweat.

Perhaps the best rain outfit is a rain poncho plus sweaters, shirts, and an unlined jacket. With the many changes in weather, you can put on or take off layers of clothes to get warm or to cool down. If it rains, your poncho will keep you dry. Backpackers and day hikers need longer ponchos to drape over their packs.

Depending on where you walk, you can use rubber boots or waterproofed hiking boots. If you just plan to take a nature walk in the Hoh Rain Forest, a rain hat with a wide brim will let you say, "Rain, rain, come my way." Then you can hear the rain thumping your hat while you count the zillion shades of green in the forest.

# Trees in Danger

As you travel Highway 101 around the outside of the park, you'll see trucks carrying big logs cut from thick forests. They're taking sitka spruce and hemlock to paper pulp mills and western redcedar to lumber mills. Douglas-fir is used for both pulp and lumber.

The logs *were not cut down in the national park.* They were cut from forests on private land or in parts of the national *forest.*

These forests seem so thick, you might think we could never run out of trees. But trees take hundreds of years to grow, so many companies that cut and sell wood also plant trees.

Western redcedar grows very slowly. Its seeds also need a wet, acid soil to sprout in. Redcedars are popular for building and are being cut down faster than new ones can grow. It will take hundreds of years for today's seedlings to reach the size of the giant trees now being cut down.

One of the biggest western redcedars stands in a grove about ten kilometers north of Kalaloch Ranger Station. It's really several trees grown together. The trunk is almost as big around as a two-car garage, and it reaches 40 meters into the sky.

**Older Western Redcedars Stand Straight And Tall**

**Young Western Redcedar**

# Wilderness – Who Needs It?

Who needs the wilderness? For the elk, deer, and cougar, it's home. Birds nest in the trees, and squirrels feast on the seeds of sitka spruce cones. Fish live in streams and the ocean and swim up rivers to mate and lay eggs. Marmots eat flowers, sedges, and herbs so they can get fat and hibernate in winter.

In the wilderness, fallen leaves and needles make a thick layer called duff. Like a sponge soaking up water, duff stores precipitation before it runs off into the ocean. Plant roots hold soil and keep the mountain from eroding away faster than it does.

Outside the park, loggers need the trees of the wilderness to make pulp for paper and lumber for building houses. They know they must plant new trees to replace the ones they cut down. Then, 50, 80, or 100 years from now, loggers will again find big trees to cut in the forest.

Because of the climate in Washington, Olympic National Park is rich in resources. Its resources are water, trees, and gifts from the ocean.

Perhaps the greatest resource is a thing you can't buy or sell. That resource is a wilderness where people can go to breathe fresh air and feel peaceful.

**Who Needs A Wilderness?** ▶

# Other Parks in Washington

MOUNT RAINIER NATIONAL PARK has the second highest peak, the biggest glacier, and the longest glacier in the United States south of Alaska.

A system of 41 glaciers crowns Mount Rainier, and heavy precipitation waters a dense forest around its base.

Many activities draw visitors to this national park: hiking, skiing, and ice and mountain climbing, as well as camping and fishing.

Geologists, the people who study the earth, find a lot to explore in NORTH CASCADES NATIONAL PARK. In this park, earth tilts, giant faults, and the remains of ancient volcanoes tell the ever-changing story of earth formations.

Heavy precipitation has produced glaciers, snowfields, ice caps, and other wonders. Visitors are also attracted by 555 kilometers of hiking and horse trails, lakes for fishing, and the exciting scenery of the "American Alps."

**Mount Rainier National Park**

**North Cascades National Park**

# The Author and Illustrator

Wyoming-born Ruth Radlauer's love for national parks began with Yellowstone. In her younger years she spent her summers in the Bighorn Mountains, at Yellowstone, or in the mountains near Casper.

Ed and Ruth Radlauer, graduates of the University of California at Los Angeles, are authors of many books for young people. Their subjects range from social studies to youth activities such as horse riding and motorcycling.

The Radlauers live in California, where they spend most of their time in the mountains near Los Angeles.

Photographing the national parks is a labor of love for Rolf Zillmer and his wife Evelyn. Because they are backpackers and wildlife enthusiasts, the Zillmers can give a truly intimate view of each park.

A former student at Art Center College of Design in Los Angeles, Mr. Zillmer was born in New York City. He now makes his home in Los Angeles, California, where he does painting, sculpture, and most of the art direction for Elk Grove Books.